I0410381

August 2014

IDENTITY THEFT

Additional Actions Could Help IRS Combat the Large, Evolving Threat of Refund Fraud

GAO-14-633

GAO Highlights

Highlights of GAO-14-633, a report to congressional requesters.

August 2014

IDENTITY THEFT

Additional Actions Could Help IRS Combat the Large, Evolving Threat of Refund Fraud

Why GAO Did This Study

Identity theft tax refund fraud is a persistent, evolving threat to honest taxpayers and tax administration. It occurs when an identity thief files a fraudulent tax return using a legitimate taxpayer's identifying information and claims a refund.

GAO was asked to review IRS's efforts to combat IDT refund fraud. This report, the first of a series, examines (1) what IRS knows about the extent of IDT refund fraud and (2) additional actions IRS can take to combat IDT refund fraud using third-party information from, for example, employers and financial institutions.

To understand what is known about the extent of IDT refund fraud, GAO reviewed IRS documentation, including the *Identity Theft Taxonomy*. To identify additional actions IRS can take, GAO assessed IRS and SSA data on the timing of W-2s; and interviewed SSA officials and selected associations representing software companies, return preparers, payroll companies, and others.

What GAO Recommends

GAO recommends that Congress should consider providing Treasury with authority to lower the annual threshold for e-filing W-2s. In addition, IRS should fully assess the costs and benefits of shifting W-2 deadlines, and provide this information to Congress. IRS neither agreed nor disagreed with GAO's recommendations, and it stated it is determining how these potential corrective actions align with available resources and IRS priorities.

View GAO-14-633. For more information, contact James R. White at (202) 512-9110 or whitej@gao.gov.

What GAO Found

Based on preliminary analysis, the Internal Revenue Service (IRS) estimates it paid $5.2 billion in fraudulent identity theft (IDT) refunds in filing season 2013, while preventing $24.2 billion (based on what it could detect). The full extent is unknown because of the challenges inherent in detecting IDT refund fraud.

IDT refund fraud takes advantage of IRS's "look-back" compliance model. Under this model, rather than holding refunds until completing all compliance checks, IRS issues refunds after conducting selected reviews. While there are no simple solutions, one option is earlier matching of employer-reported wage information to taxpayers' returns before issuing refunds. IRS currently cannot do such matching because employers' wage data (from Form W-2s) are not available until months after IRS issues most refunds. Consequently, IRS begins matching employer-reported W-2 data to tax returns in July, following the tax season. If IRS had access to W-2 data earlier—through accelerated W-2 deadlines and increased electronic filing of W-2s—it could conduct pre-refund matching and identify discrepancies to prevent the issuance of billions in fraudulent refunds.

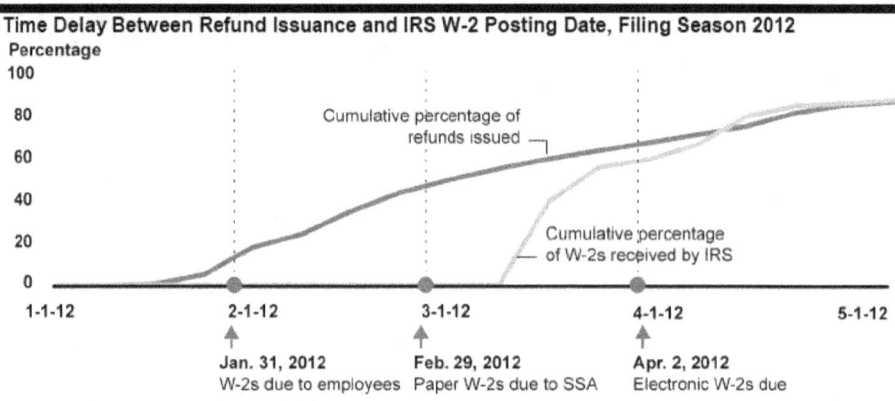

Time Delay Between Refund Issuance and IRS W-2 Posting Date, Filing Season 2012

Source: GAO analysis of IRS data | GAO-14-633

Accelerated W-2 deadlines. In 2014, the Department of the Treasury (Treasury) proposed that Congress accelerate W-2 deadlines to January 31. However, IRS has not fully assessed the impacts of this proposal. Without this assessment, Congress does not have the information needed to deliberate the merits of such a significant change to W-2 deadlines or the use of pre-refund W-2 matching. Such an assessment is consistent with IRS's strategic plan that calls for analytics-based decisions, and would help IRS ensure effective use of resources.

Increased e-filing of W-2s. Treasury has requested authority to reduce the 250-return threshold for electronically filing (e-filing) information returns. The Social Security Administration (SSA) estimated that to meaningfully increase W-2 e-filing, the threshold would have to be lowered to include those filing 5 to 10 W-2s. In addition, SSA estimated an administrative cost savings of about $0.50 per e-filed W-2. Based on these cost savings and the ancillary benefits they provide in supporting IRS's efforts to conduct more pre-refund matching, a change in the e-filing threshold is warranted. Without this change, some employers' paper W-2s could not be available for IRS matching until much later in the year, due to the additional time needed to process paper forms.

_____ United States Government Accountability Office

Contents

Figures

Abbreviations

CDW	Compliance Data Warehouse
DDb	Dependent Database
EFDS	Electronic Fraud Detection System
e-file	electronically file
IDT	identity theft
IP PIN	Identity Protection Personal Identification Number
IRS	Internal Revenue Service
RRP	Return Review Program
SSA	Social Security Administration
SSN	Social Security number
Taxonomy	IRS *Identity Theft Taxonomy*
Treasury	Department of the Treasury
W-2	Form W-2, *Wage and Tax Statement*
W-2c	Form W-2c, *Corrected Wage and Tax Statement*

GAO

U.S. GOVERNMENT ACCOUNTABILITY OFFICE

441 G St. N.W.
Washington, DC 20548

August 20, 2014

The Honorable Ron Wyden
Chairman
The Honorable Orrin Hatch
Ranking Member
Committee on Finance
United States Senate

The Honorable Bill Nelson
Chairman
The Honorable Susan M. Collins
Ranking Member
Special Committee on Aging
United States Senate

The Honorable Dave Camp
Chairman
Committee on Ways and Means
House of Representatives

Tax refund fraud associated with identity theft (IDT) continues to be an evolving threat, one that imposes a serious financial and emotional toll on honest taxpayers and threatens the integrity of the tax administration system. Within the tax system, IDT refund fraud occurs when a refund-seeking identity thief files a fraudulent tax return using a legitimate taxpayer's identifying information. The Internal Revenue Service (IRS) estimates that millions of IDT refund fraud attempts claiming tens of billions of dollars in fraudulent refunds occurred in 2013. IDT refund fraud also creates administrative costs: In 2014, IRS has approximately 3,000 people working on cases of IDT victims—more than twice the number of people working on these cases in 2011. In light of this, IRS recognized refund fraud and IDT as a major challenge affecting the agency in its recently issued strategic plan.[1]

To craft a response to IDT refund fraud, IRS must understand the extent and nature of the fraud. In 2012, we reported that IRS managers did not

---

[1] IRS, *Strategic Plan: FY2014-2017*, (Washington, D.C.: 2014).

have a complete picture.[2] For example, IRS did not know the full extent of IDT refund fraud, nor did IRS systematically track the characteristics of known identity theft tax returns. While complete knowledge about identities stolen and perpetrators responsible will likely never be attained, the more thoroughly IRS understands the problem, the more effectively IRS and policymakers can respond.

IRS has taken a number of steps to address this threat, including developing an estimate of the extent of IDT refund fraud and using third-party information (such as leads about suspicious refunds) to help in its IDT efforts. However, available information suggests that the problem is persistent and evolving.

Within this context, you asked us to examine IRS's efforts to combat IDT refund fraud, which we will review in a series of reports. This report answers the following questions:

1. What does IRS know about the extent of IDT refund fraud?
2. What additional actions can IRS take to combat IDT refund fraud using third-party information (for example, from employers and financial institutions)?

A report to be issued later in 2014 will address a broader set of actions that IRS could take to combat IDT refund fraud.

To understand what IRS knows about the extent of IDT refund fraud, we reviewed IRS's *Identity Theft Taxonomy (Taxonomy)*—a matrix of IDT refund fraud categories—which estimates the amount of IDT refund fraud that IRS is, and is not, preventing. We conducted manual data testing for obvious errors and compared underlying data to IRS's *Refund Fraud & Identity Theft Global Report*. We confirmed *Taxonomy* components where we had data available to cross check. We also interviewed IRS officials to better understand the methodology used to create the estimates. For a summary of *Taxonomy* limitations, see appendix I.

To identify opportunities to improve IRS's IDT refund fraud efforts, we reviewed *Internal Revenue Manual* sections detailing IRS's Identity

---

[2]GAO, *Identity Theft: Total Extent of Refund Fraud Using Stolen Identities is Unknown*, GAO-13-132T (Washington, D.C.: Nov. 29, 2012).

Protection Program and IRS documentation for its External Leads Program (where third parties, often financial institutions, report suspicious refunds to IRS), Opt-In Program (where financial institutions can flag and reject suspicious refunds sent via direct deposit), and other third-party efforts. We interviewed officials from the Social Security Administration (SSA) and from associations representing software companies, return preparers, financial institutions, and payroll companies. To help ensure our analysis covered a variety of viewpoints, we selected a nonprobability sample of 22 associations and stakeholders with differing positions and characteristics, based on IRS documentation and suggestions, prior GAO work, and other information. Because we used a nonprobability sample, the views of these associations are not generalizable to all potential third parties. We then communicated with IRS offices, including (1) Privacy, Government Liaison, and Disclosure; and (2) Return Integrity and Correspondence Services, to determine the feasibility of various options and the challenges of pursuing them. See appendix II for details on our scope and methodology.

We conducted this performance audit from May 2014 to August 2014 in accordance with generally accepted government auditing standards. Those standards require that we plan and perform the audit to obtain sufficient, appropriate evidence to provide a reasonable basis for our findings and conclusions based on our audit objectives. We believe that the evidence obtained provides a reasonable basis for our findings and conclusions based on our audit objectives.

Background

IRS has reported a substantial increase in IDT refund fraud; however, it is unclear whether this reported increase is due to an overall increase in IDT refund fraud, to an improvement in IRS's ability to detect IDT refund fraud, or to a combination of the two. For example, IRS instituted IDT filters in 2012, which helped IRS find additional IDT incidents, but it is not known how much of the reported increase can be attributed to filters or to an increase in IDT refund fraud.

There are two types of tax-related IDT fraud: (1) refund fraud and (2) employment fraud. IDT refund fraud occurs when a refund-seeking identity thief files a fraudulent tax return using the legitimate taxpayer's identifying information. Employment fraud occurs when an identity thief uses a taxpayer's name and Social Security number (SSN) to obtain a job. This report's discussion focuses on IDT refund fraud and not employment fraud.

IDT refund fraud takes advantage of the typical process of filing a tax return. Taxpayers receive information returns from third parties, such as the Form W-2, *Wage and Tax Statement* (W-2), and use this information to complete their tax returns. As shown in figure 1, taxpayers with wage income typically receive a Form W-2 from their employer by late January. Taxpayers copy the information from the W-2 to prepare their returns. Taxpayers filing paper returns are required to attach a copy of the W-2 to the return. Taxpayers filing electronically (e-file), as most do, are not required to send W-2s to the IRS. Most taxpayers entitled to a refund, along with many identity thieves attempting refund fraud, file early in the filing season—many in February. During return processing, IRS performs some compliance checks and issues refunds, but at this time it cannot verify the W-2 information for all returns (paper W-2s can be forged and fictitious wage information can be entered on a tax return).[3] By the end of March, employers are also required to send a copy of the W-2 to SSA, which performs verification checks before sending the information to IRS.[4] However, IRS only begins matching W-2 information from employers to tax returns in July. This gap between when IRS issues refunds and when IRS matches W-2s to tax returns creates the opportunity for fraudsters to file returns using a stolen identity and to receive a tax refund.

---

[3]In certain instances, IRS requests W-2 information from employers to validate information on returns selected by fraud filters.

[4]Employers must provide W-2s to employees by January 31 and to SSA by February 29 (for paper W-2s) and March 31 (for e-filed W-2s).

Figure 1: Example of the Typical Process for Filing a Tax Return

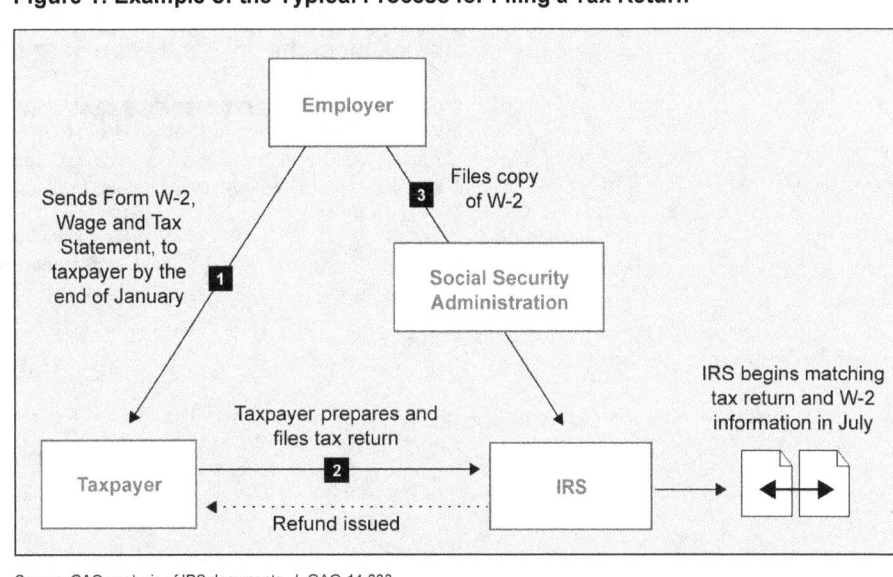

Source: GAO analysis of IRS documents. | GAO-14-633

Issuing refunds before fully verifying the information on tax returns is an example of what IRS officials refer to as a "look-back" compliance model: rather than holding refunds until all compliance checks can be completed, IRS issues refunds after doing some selected, automated reviews of the information the taxpayer submits to verify identity (e.g., name and SSN matching); filtering out returns with indicators of fraud such as a mismatched name and SSN; and correcting obvious errors, such as calculation mistakes and claims for credits and deductions exceeding statutory limits. IRS's intent is to issue refunds quickly.[5]

After refunds are issued, IRS does further checks. Two of these checks enable IRS to detect significant amounts of IDT refund fraud after the fact. One, shown at the top of figure 2, is checking for duplicate returns. If an identity thief and a legitimate taxpayer file returns using the same name and SSN, IRS will have duplicate returns. The other is matching tax returns to third-party information provided to IRS by employers, financial

---

[5]For 2014, IRS informed taxpayers that it would generally issue refunds in less than 21 days after receiving a tax return. IRS is required by law to pay interest if it takes longer than 45 days after the due date of the return to issue a refund. 26 U.S.C. § 6611(e).

institutions, and others (bottom of figure 2). Matching tax returns to W-2s is an example of these checks. As we have reported, these post-refund compliance checks can take a year or more to complete.[6]

Figure 2: Examples of Identity Theft Refund Fraud That IRS Detects

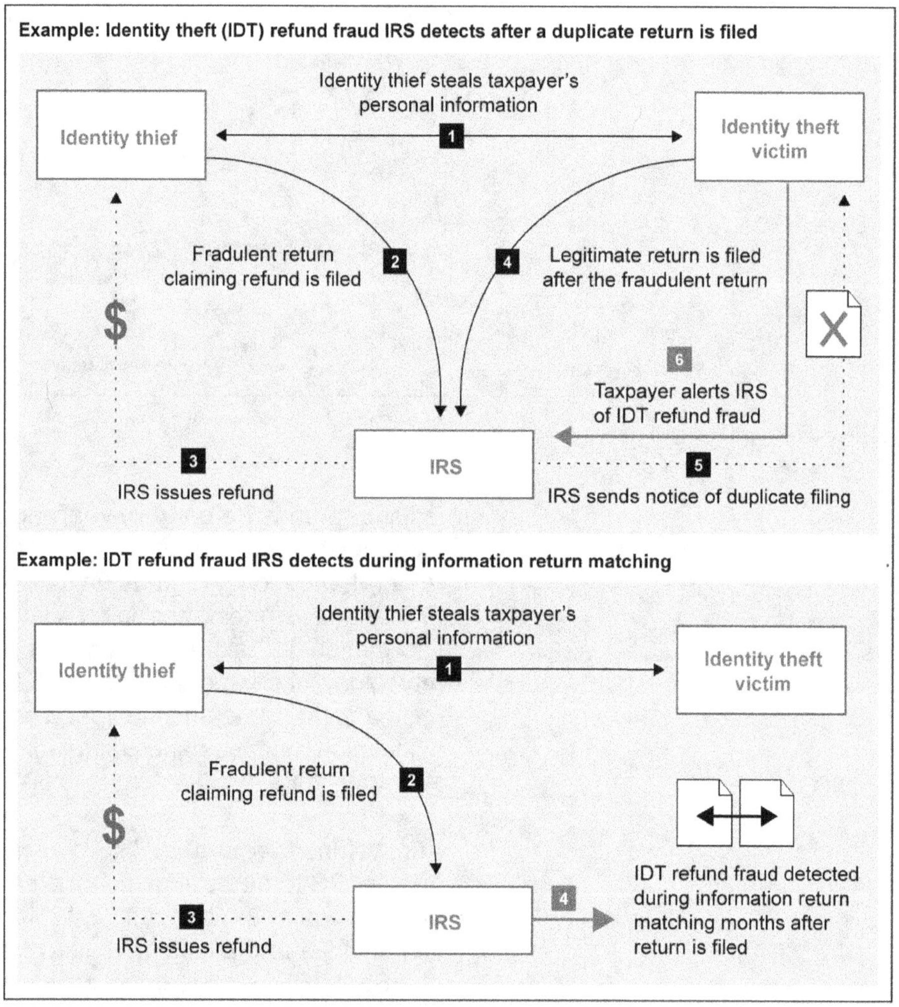

Example: Identity theft (IDT) refund fraud IRS detects after a duplicate return is filed

Identity thief steals taxpayer's personal information **1**

Identity thief

Identity theft victim

Fradulent return claiming refund is filed **2**

4 Legitimate return is filed after the fraudulent return

$

6 Taxpayer alerts IRS of IDT refund fraud

3 IRS issues refund

IRS

5 IRS sends notice of duplicate filing

Example: IDT refund fraud IRS detects during information return matching

Identity thief steals taxpayer's personal information **1**

Identity thief

Identity theft victim

Fradulent return claiming refund is filed **2**

$

3 IRS issues refund

IRS

4 IDT refund fraud detected during information return matching months after return is filed

Source: GAO analysis of IRS documents. | GAO-14-633

Note: Numbers represent the order in which these actions occur in the examples.

---

[6]GAO, *Tax Refunds: IRS is Exploring Verification Improvements, but Needs to Better Manage Risks,* GAO-13-515 (Washington, D.C.: June 4, 2013).

IRS Tools to Combat Identity Theft Refund Fraud

Recognizing the limitations of the look-back compliance model, IRS's efforts to combat IDT refund fraud occur at three different stages of the refund process: (1) before accepting a tax return, (2) during tax return processing, and (3) after issuing tax refunds. At each stage of the process, IRS uses specific tools to detect IDT refund fraud (see figure 3 for examples of IRS tools at each stage).

Figure 3: Examples of IRS Tools Used to Combat Identity Theft Refund Fraud, by Processing Stage

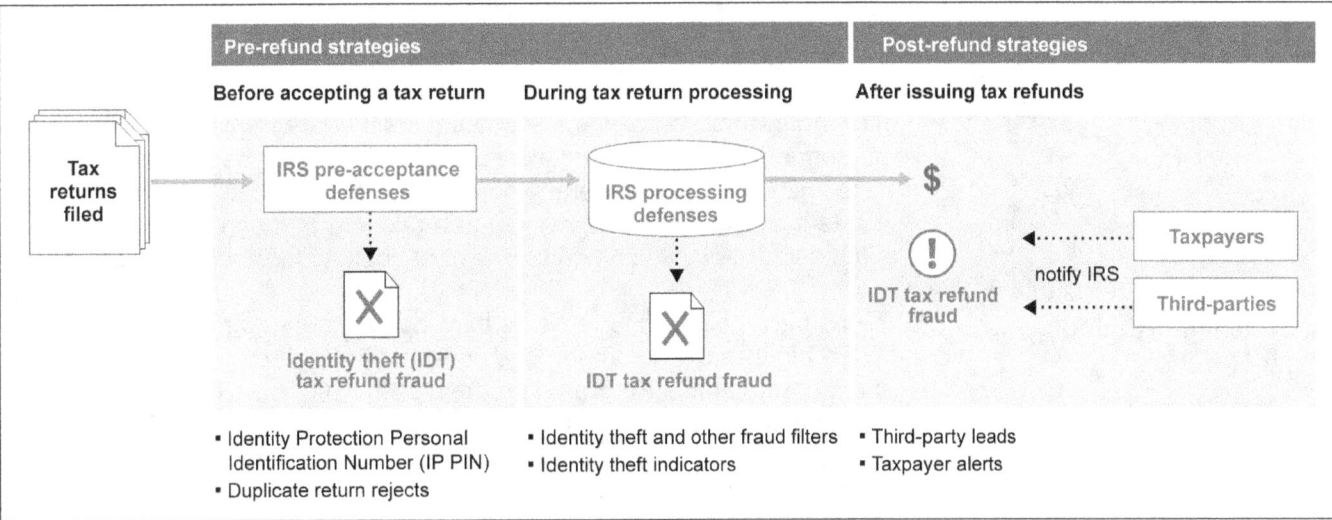

Source: GAO analysis of IRS information. | GAO-14-633

Before Accepting a Tax Return (Pre-Acceptance)

Identity Protection Personal Identification Number (IP PIN). IP PINs are single-use identification numbers sent to IDT victims who have validated their identities with IRS. Tax returns with IP PINs pass through IRS's IDT fraud filters, avoiding false positives—where a legitimate taxpayer is identified as an identity thief—and a delayed tax refund. Taxpayers who were issued an IP PIN but e-filed without using it or entered it incorrectly are prompted to enter the IP PIN on their tax return or to file on paper, according to IRS officials. Paper returns filed with the SSN of these taxpayers and without an IP PIN are subject to additional checks. (In January 2014, IRS offered a limited IP PIN pilot program to eligible taxpayers in Florida, Georgia, and the District of Columbia.)

Duplicate return rejects. Once IRS receives an e-filed return for a given SSN, it automatically rejects subsequent returns filed using that SSN and sends a notice of duplicate filing, as shown at the top of figure 2.[7]

During Tax Return Processing

IDT and other fraud filters. IDT filters screen returns, using characteristics that IRS has identified in previous IDT refund fraud schemes.[8] The filters also search for clusters of returns with similar characteristics, such as the same bank account or address, which could indicate potential fraud. If an IDT filter flags a return, IRS stops processing the return and sends a letter asking the taxpayer to validate his or her identity.

IDT indicators. Indicators—account flags that are visible to all IRS personnel with account access—are a key tool IRS uses to resolve and detect IDT. IRS uses different indicators (e.g., to denote whether the incident was identified by the IRS or a taxpayer), depending on the circumstances in which IRS learns of an identity theft-related problem.

After Issuing Refunds (Post-Refund)

Third-party leads. IRS receives third-party leads regarding suspected IDT refund fraud and other types of refund fraud through efforts including the External Leads Program and the Opt-In Program. The External Leads Program involves third parties providing lead information to IRS. If a questionable refund is confirmed as fraudulent, IRS requests that the financial institution return the refund. The Opt-In Program allows financial institutions to electronically reject suspicious refunds and return them to IRS, indicating why the institution is rejecting the refunds.

Taxpayer alerts. IRS often identifies IDT refund fraud after receiving a phone call from a taxpayer who cannot file because an identity thief already filed with the SSN (i.e., a duplicate return) or because the taxpayer received a notice from IRS. For example, IRS can discover IDT when a taxpayer responds to an IRS compliance notice stating that the

---

[7]If a subsequent return using the SSN is filed on paper, IRS systems detect the return during processing.

[8]Two of the tax-administration systems employing filters are the Dependent Database (DDb) and Electronic Fraud Detection System (EFDS). DDb incorporates IRS, Health & Human Services, and Social Security Administration data to identify compliance issues involving IDT, refundable credits, and prisoners. EFDS is a legacy system built in the mid-1990s. To replace EFDS, IRS is developing the Return Review Program.

IRS has income and/or payment information that does not match the information reported by the taxpayer on his return.

Performance Management Information and Controls Help Agencies Assure Results and Best Use of Federal Resources

A key practice in results-oriented management of federal agencies is the establishment of agency-wide, long-term strategic goals. IRS's strategic plan for fiscal years 2014-2017 identifies two strategic goals: (1) deliver high quality and timely service to reduce taxpayer burden and encourage voluntary compliance and (2) effectively enforce the law to ensure compliance with tax responsibilities and combat fraud. The strategic plan also outlines several objectives relevant to its efforts to combat identity theft, including

- strengthening refund fraud prevention by balancing the speed of refund delivery with the assurance of taxpayer identity, using analysis of third-party and historical taxpayer data, and educating taxpayers and tax professionals on fraud risk factors and fraud prevention methods;

- implementing enterprise-wide analytics and research capabilities to make timely, informed decisions; and

- implementing and maintaining a robust enterprise risk management program, which includes establishing routine reporting procedures to external stakeholders on operational risks.

As a complement to the potential benefits of strategic planning, internal control is a major part of managing an organization.[9] Internal control comprises the plans, methods, and procedures used to meet missions, goals, and objectives: this supports performance-based management. Internal control helps agency program managers achieve desired results and provides reasonable assurance that program objectives are being achieved through—among other things—effective and efficient use of agency resources. Managers are to design internal controls based on related costs and benefits. In addition, internal control standards in the federal government call for agencies to record and communicate relevant, reliable, and timely information on internal and external events to agency managers and others who need it.

---

[9]GAO, *Standards for Internal Control in the Federal Government,* GAO/AIMD-00-21.3.1 (Washington, D.C.: Nov. 1, 1999).

In Filing Season 2013, IRS Estimates Paying $5.2 Billion in Fraudulent IDT Refunds While Preventing $24.2 Billion; However, the Full Extent of IDT Refund Fraud Is Unknown

Based on IRS's preliminary *Identity Theft Taxonomy (Taxonomy)*, the agency estimated that $29.4 billion in IDT refund fraud was attempted in filing season 2013. IRS estimated it prevented or recovered about $24.2 billion (82 percent) of the estimated attempted refund fraud. However, IRS estimated it paid $5.2 billion (18 percent) in IDT refunds during the same timeframe (see figure 4). IRS officials noted that they are updating their analysis and anticipate revising the *Taxonomy's* estimate of IDT refunds paid. The officials said the revised estimates could be somewhat higher (perhaps by $0.6 billion) but the analysis was not completed in time for us to include it in figure 4.

Figure 4: IRS Preliminary Estimates of Attempted Identity Theft Refund Fraud, Filing Season 2013

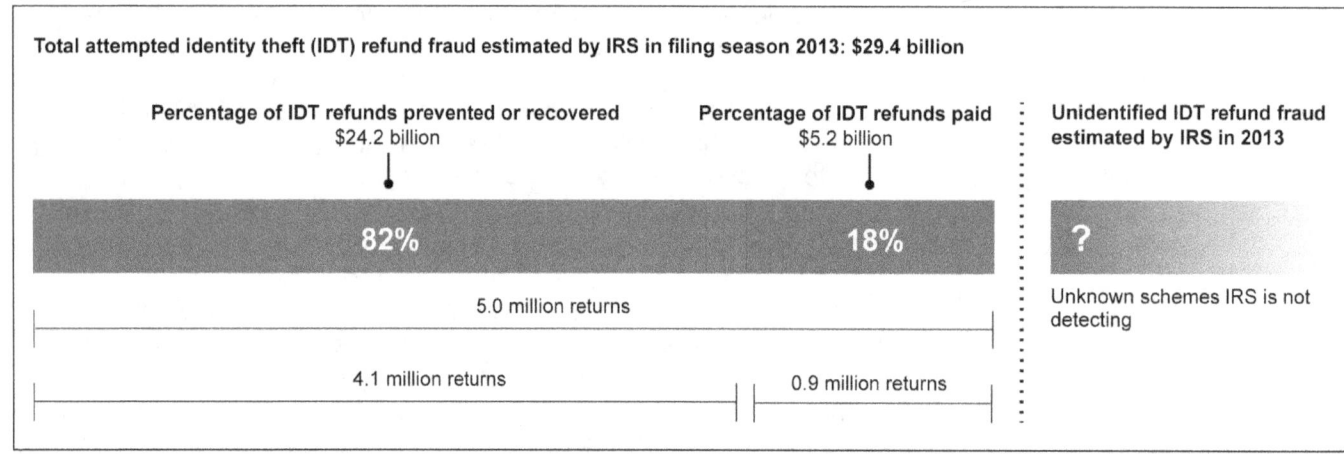

Source: GAO analysis of IRS data. | GAO-14-633

Note: IRS officials are updating their analysis and anticipate revising the estimate of IDT refunds paid.

IRS's *Taxonomy* demonstrates a significant effort on the part of IRS and is an important first step in estimating how much *identified* IDT refund fraud IRS is stopping or failing to stop. IRS has made substantial progress in its efforts to estimate IDT refund fraud. For example, IRS developed an estimate of IDT refund fraud by identifying characteristics of fraudulent returns, matching and analyzing information returns and tax returns based on these characteristics, and researching other sources.

However, the estimates will continue to evolve as IRS updates its methodology to better reflect new IDT refund fraud schemes and to improve the accuracy of its estimates, according to IRS officials.[10]

IRS's *Taxonomy* is a valuable tool to help inventory, characterize, and analyze available IDT refund fraud data and to assess the performance of IRS's IDT refund fraud defenses. For example, the *Taxonomy* may help IRS

- **Monitor progress.** Given the evolving, persistent nature of IDT refund fraud, IRS will constantly need to monitor and adapt its IDT defenses to protect against new and emerging schemes. The *Taxonomy* provides IRS with a methodology for monitoring IDT refund fraud and the progress of IRS defenses over time. However, IRS will continue to face challenges in evaluating its defenses. For example, it is difficult to differentiate whether an increase in returns detected by the IDT filters is due to improved filter performance or to an increase in the overall number of IDT refund fraud attempts. In addition, future methodology updates which reflect evolving schemes and improve accuracy could make comparisons between filing seasons difficult.

- **Identify schemes.** The *Taxonomy* may help IRS develop a better understanding of taxpayer characteristics related to current, successful IDT refund fraud, including filing status, the size of the refund, filing method, and filing history. This could help IRS identify IDT refund fraud scheme trends and assist it in further developing and modifying its defenses.

- **Communicate the extent of the problem to stakeholders.** While the *Taxonomy* has limitations, it may help improve IRS managers' understanding of the problem, allowing them to better communicate with policymakers about schemes and resource needs. It may also improve the ability of Congress (and other decision makers) to oversee IRS's efforts. In addition, the data collected could be of use to IRS partners, including tax preparers and financial institutions.

---

[10]During the course of our audit, we found that IRS's methodology for counting returns did not include two categories of duplicate returns that should have been included in the estimates. IRS officials estimated that including these returns would increase IRS's original 2013 estimates of refunds paid out by $0.47 billion, from $4.75 billion to $5.22 billion in filing season 2013.

Although IRS's *Taxonomy* estimates are valuable in helping estimate IDT refund fraud, they are, by their nature, incomplete. This is in part because IRS's estimate of IDT refunds paid (the $5.2 billion shown in figure 4) is based on duplicate returns, information return mismatches, and criminal investigations identified after the refunds are paid. However, for cases where there are no duplicate returns, information returns, or criminal investigations associated with a tax return, IRS has been unable to estimate the amount of IDT refund fraud (the *unidentified* IDT refund fraud shown in figure 4). Also, certain *Taxonomy* estimates are based on assumptions using the characteristics of past IDT refund fraud. While the assumptions are based on IRS's research from known cases and appear reasonable, we could not verify the accuracy and comprehensiveness of these assumptions. This is because the accuracy of the *Taxonomy* estimates is largely based on whether the estimate includes all true IDT refund fraud returns and excludes all legitimate returns. IRS officials acknowledged their estimates for returns flagged during information return matching could include legitimate returns that are not actual IDT refund fraud.

Other limitations[11] that we identified in the *Taxonomy* include the following:

- **The *Taxonomy* underestimates the number of IDT refund fraud returns and refund amounts for some IDT categories and overestimates others.** The *Taxonomy* underestimates IDT refund fraud because, as previously discussed, IRS has been unable to estimate the amount of IDT refund fraud for cases where there are no criminal investigations, duplicate returns, or information returns—such as a W-2—associated with a tax return (the *unidentified* IDT refund fraud shown in figure 4). An example of an overestimated category is that of "refunds recovered," which includes refunds returned to IRS as a result of external leads. However, IRS data on external leads do not distinguish whether the type of fraud was IDT refund fraud or some other type of fraud. Our analysis of the *Taxonomy* found that IRS did not adjust its estimate to account for other types of refund fraud.

- **While IRS provided *Taxonomy* estimates for filing seasons 2012 and 2013, methodology changes make it difficult to compare these estimates over time.** For example, the filing season 2013

---

[11]See appendix I for additional details on limitations.

estimate uses a different data source to estimate the number of IDT refunds paid and eventually detected after the filing season (when IRS matches tax returns to information return data, such as W-2s). In addition, it is unclear whether changes in the number of IDT refund fraud returns are due to overall changes in fraud patterns, such as an increase or decrease in fraud attempts; to improvements in IRS IDT defenses; or to identity thieves' ability to file returns using schemes IRS has not yet learned to detect.

Stronger Pre-refund and Post-refund Strategies Can Help Combat IDT Refund Fraud

IRS has responded to the problem of IDT refund fraud with new ways to combat fraud. However, according to IRS officials, identity thieves are "adaptive adversaries" who are constantly learning and changing their tactics as IRS develops new IDT strategies. Therefore, IDT refund fraud remains a persistent, evolving threat that requires stronger pre-refund and post-refund strategies to combat.

A robust pre-refund strategy is important because preventing fraudulent refunds is easier and more cost-effective than trying to recover them after they have been issued. We have previously reported that implementing strong preventive controls can help defend against invalid payments, increasing public confidence and avoiding the difficult "pay and chase" aspects of recovering invalid refunds.[12] According to IRS, the agency's Return Review Program (RRP) is one way that IRS is trying to improve its pre-refund detection efforts.[13] As IRS processes tax returns, other strategies can assist in identifying and stopping suspicious refunds. Moreover, improving post-refund programs may help IRS work with financial institutions to stop refunds that earlier controls have missed. However, recapturing a fraudulent refund after it is issued can be challenging—if not impossible—because identity thieves often spend or transfer the funds immediately, making them very difficult to trace.

---

[12]GAO, *Improper Payments: Remaining Challenges and Strategies for Governmentwide Reduction Efforts*, GAO-12-573T (Washington, D.C.: Mar. 28, 2012).

[13]RRP is intended to be a web-based automated system designed to enhance IRS's capabilities to detect, resolve, and prevent criminal and civil noncompliance. While IRS recently launched an initial version of RRP to run parallel with EFDS, IRS officials told us that the next version is on a "strategic pause" while IRS officials clarify RRP's functionality.

Agency officials and third-party stakeholders we spoke to identified the following potential pre- and post-refund strategies that may help IRS combat IDT refund fraud:

- **Pre-refund.** Improve W-2 matching by (1) adjusting W-2 deadlines, (2) lowering the threshold for e-filed W-2s,[14] (3) delaying refunds, and (4) delaying the filing season.

- **Post-refund.** Improve external leads programs by providing timely, accurate, and actionable feedback to third parties.

Earlier, Pre-refund W-2 Matching May Prevent Billions of Dollars in Estimated IDT Refund Fraud but Would Involve Costs

Characteristics of the current tax processing system hamper IRS's ability to effectively verify taxpayer information prior to issuing refunds. As part of a broader proposal, the Department of the Treasury (Treasury) has proposed accelerating W-2 deadlines. This proposal will help ensure that IRS has accurate, timely W-2 data to conduct pre-refund matching. IRS has also requested funding to support timelier processing of W-2s.

IRS issues most refunds before it has access to employers' W-2 data. IRS issues most refunds months before receiving and matching information returns, such as W-2s. For 2012, IRS received more than 148.3 million tax returns and issued more than $309.6 billion in refunds to 110.5 million taxpayers. By March 1, 2012 IRS had issued about 50 percent of all 2012 refunds, but did not have access to most of the 2012 W-2 data verified by the Social Security Administration (SSA) (see figure 5).[15] As previously noted, IRS's look-back compliance model does not allow it to match tax returns to information returns until early summer.

---

[14]Currently, employers who file 250 or more W-2s annually must e-file those forms. 26 C.F.R. § 301.6011-2(b)(2). IRS is generally prohibited from requiring those filing fewer than 250 returns annually to e-file. 26 U.S.C. § 6011(e)(2)(A).

[15]We used analysis from GAO-13-515, which included data on the timing of W-2s and tax returns. SSA transmits wage data to IRS immediately upon receiving electronic W-2s, according to SSA officials. Paper W-2s require manual handling and therefore have a significantly longer processing time.

Figure 5: Time Delay Between Refund Issuance and IRS W-2 Posting Date, Filing Season 2012

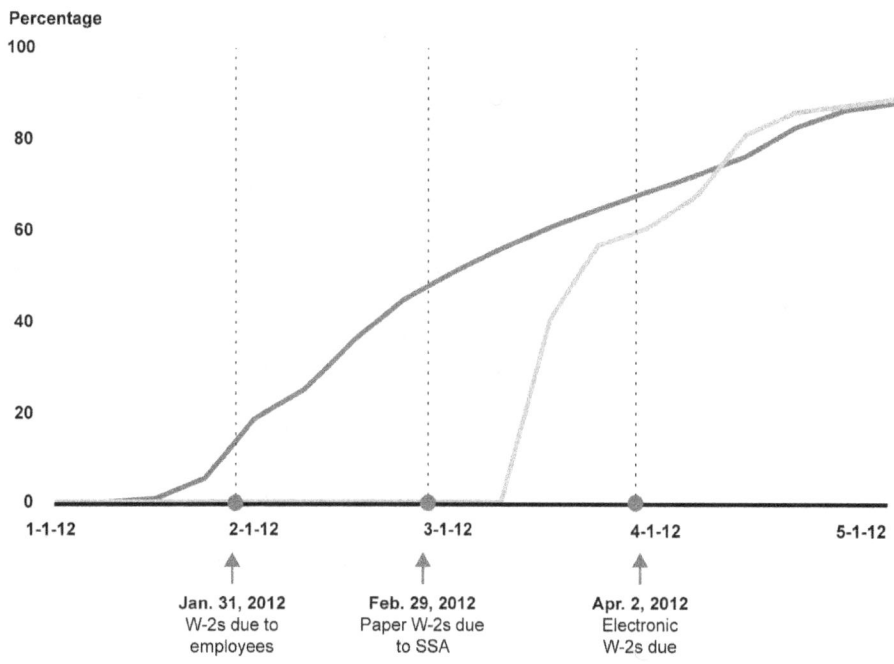

Jan. 31, 2012
W-2s due to
employees

Feb. 29, 2012
Paper W-2s due
to SSA

Apr. 2, 2012
Electronic
W-2s due

.... Cumulative percentage of W-2s received by IRS

━━━━━━ Cumulative percentage of refunds issued

Source: GAO analysis of IRS data. | GAO 14 633

Note: Due dates in filing season 2012 differed because March 31, 2012 (the electronic filing deadline) fell on a Saturday. Dates in this figure refer to the date when IRS posts tax return data to the master file, which represents when the tax return data are available for matching. Officials noted that IRS must refine the data prior to posting to IRS systems. This may include identifying and correcting incomplete or inaccurate data before posting the data to IRS systems.

IRS is under pressure to issue refunds promptly. IRS is required by law to pay interest if it takes longer than 45 days after the due date of the return to issue a refund.[16] IRS informs taxpayers to anticipate their refunds generally within 21 days after filing and actively tries to meet this target. For tax year 2013, IRS reported that for tax returns filed through

---

[16]26 U.S.C. § 6611(e).

early March, taxpayers received refunds an average of 9.6 days after filing.[17]

Treasury's Proposal for Accelerated W-2 Deadlines is Intended to Benefit IRS and Taxpayers

To facilitate the use of W-2 information in detection of noncompliance (which includes IDT refund fraud) earlier in the filing season, Treasury recently proposed to Congress that the W-2 deadlines be moved to January 31 (for both paper and e-filing).[18] IRS also requested funding for processing W-2s more quickly as part of its fiscal year 2015 budget request.[19] The IRS Commissioner has also advocated for earlier deadlines, testifying that challenges with IDT refund fraud have led IRS to propose an accelerated W-2 filing deadline.[20] Further, the National Taxpayer Advocate has repeatedly written about the need to develop an accelerated information reporting system to enable IRS to match third-party reports to return data before issuing refunds.[21]

According to IRS officials, earlier, pre-refund W-2 matching would provide a number of benefits, including

- **Combating IDT refund fraud.** According to IRS officials, having earlier access to W-2s, and time to match W-2s to tax returns before issuing refunds, would give IRS more opportunities to prevent billions

---

[17]Estimated based on 99 percent of all refund returns.

[18]Treasury, *General Explanations of the Administration's Fiscal Year 2015 Revenue Proposals,* (Washington, D.C.: Mar. 2014). Each February, Treasury releases this publication in conjunction with the President's budget. As part of its proposal to stagger tax return filing dates, Treasury proposed implementing an accelerated deadline for filing information returns and eliminating the extended due date for e-filed returns. Under the proposal, paper and e-filed W-2s would be due to SSA by January 31, the same date W-2s are due to employees.

[19]IRS, *Fiscal Year 2015 President's Budget,* (Washington, D.C.). IRS requested $21.6 million and 51 full time equivalents to fund five information technology projects, including a project to improve access to SSA data.

[20]John Koskinen, Commissioner of Internal Revenue, oral testimony before the Senate Appropriations Subcommittee on Financial Services and General Government, 113th Cong., Apr. 30, 2014.

[21]See, for example, National Taxpayer Advocate, *2013 Annual Report to Congress*, Vol. II: (Washington, D.C.: Dec. 31, 2013).

of dollars of IDT refund fraud.[22] Returns flagged during IRS's information return matching make up a substantial portion of the $5.2 billion in IDT refunds that IRS estimated it paid in filing season 2013, according to IRS's *Taxonomy*. With earlier access to W-2 data, IRS could validate information reported on a tax return (e.g., wages and compensation) with information reported by employers before issuing refunds.[23] Even without automatic matching, IRS officials said that earlier W-2 data would speed up manual reviews of high-risk returns—such such as those flagged by the IDT filters—because the information they rely on to perform those checks would be readily available.

- **Benefiting taxpayers and employers.** In addition to protecting revenue, accelerated W-2 reporting and pre-refund matching could improve taxpayer service and reduce burden. IRS officials said that having W-2 data at the beginning of the filing season would reduce taxpayer burden by allowing IRS to verify income immediately and to release legitimate tax returns caught by the IDT filters (false positives). Earlier W-2 data could also help IRS reduce employer burden, as IRS would no longer have to contact employers of taxpayers whose returns are flagged by IDT and other fraud filters.

- **Providing other benefits.** Earlier W-2 matching could reduce IRS's workload of collection cases and help taxpayers avoid penalties and interest on under-paid taxes, according to IRS officials.

Accelerated W-2 Deadlines Could Create Other Challenges that Would Need to be Addressed

Implementing accelerated W-2 deadlines could result in an increased number of corrected W-2s filed as well as other technical and logistical challenges. SSA officials and all three payroll and information reporting associations we interviewed told us that accelerating the W-2 deadline would increase the number of corrected W-2s.[24] (These are W-2s that

---

[22]While IRS could conduct pre-refund matching using other types of information returns (such as Forms 1099), we focus on W-2s in this report because IRS officials and third parties we spoke with discussed the Form W-2 as a specific tool for combating IDT refund fraud.

[23]According to IRS officials, under the current pre-refund process, IRS only uses employer-reported W-2 data to verify information on returns selected by fraud filters (about 1 percent of all returns IRS receives). To perform these verification checks, IRS contacts individual employers to verify wage and withholding information.

[24]Employers file Form W-2c, *Corrected Wage and Tax Statements* (W-2c), when they need to make changes to previously submitted W-2s. For example, employers may file W-2cs to correct errors reported by employees.

employers correct after sending the first incorrect version to SSA.) Corrected W-2s represent less than 1 percent of the 213.5 million W-2s IRS received from SSA in tax year 2011, according to IRS data. The correction rate is currently low because the deadlines for filing with SSA are well after the January 31 deadline for sending W-2s to employees, giving employers a window of time to make corrections before they file with SSA. Based on data tracking payroll submissions and subsequent adjustments, the National Payroll Reporting Consortium estimated that should the deadline be accelerated to before January 31, corrections may increase from 1 percent of filed W-2s to greater than 6 percent.[25] To mitigate potential corrections, SSA officials and all three payroll and information reporting associations we interviewed recommended allowing a corrections window of time (e.g., 1 to 2 weeks) between submission to employees and to SSA.

While most W-2s are filed in a timely manner, SSA currently receives some W-2s after the March 31 deadline for submitting e-filed returns.[26] For tax year 2012, SSA received 16 percent (36.5 million of 233.2 million) of W-2s after April 5, 2013.[27] According to SSA officials, employers may submit W-2s to SSA after the filing deadline for several reasons, including (for example) human error, resubmittal of an e-filed submission previously rejected by SSA, or to report back pay under a court order. In addition, according to SSA officials, moving deadlines to January 31 or earlier would create logistical and technical challenges for SSA; however, moving the e-file deadline up to the end of February would not create issues. For example, SSA officials told us that moving the deadline to January 31 or earlier would require shifting its software development cycle because SSA's computer experts are working on another system

---

[25]National Payroll Reporting Consortium, Inc. (NPRC), *Internal Revenue Service Public Hearing: Proposed Real-Time Tax System*, (Washington, D.C.: Jan. 25, 2012). To provide information about the potential volume of corrected W-2s arising from an earlier deadline, NPRC analyzed payroll firm data on client submissions at the end of each quarter and subsequent adjustments submitted after the cutoff dates. NPRC did not analyze the impact of a January 31 deadline but based on this analysis, an NPRC official indicated a January 31 deadline would not dramatically increase corrections from current levels.

[26]Employers must submit W-2 forms to employees by January 31 and to SSA by February 29 (if filing on paper) and March 31 (if e-filing).

[27]SSA provided weekly data on W-2s. April 5, 2013 was the Friday following the March 31, 2013 deadline for e-filing W-2s.

during that timeframe; however, the computer experts are available to implement an accelerated W-2 filing date of February 29.

The Costs and Benefits of Accelerated W-2 Deadlines and Pre-refund Matching Have Not Been Assessed Fully

While Treasury and IRS officials have proposed moving up W-2 deadlines, the costs and benefits have not been identified, estimated, or documented. How IRS decides to implement pre-refund matching using W-2 data would affect the costs and benefits for itself and other stakeholders. Some of the stakeholder issues that we identified and that remain unaddressed include the following:

- **IRS**. IRS has not identified cost-effective options for updating the information technology systems or work processes (such as the process for correcting refund amounts if mismatches are detected) needed to implement pre-refund matching using W-2 data. IRS officials said that a lack of budgetary resources is the primary reason IRS has not conducted planning and analysis of the costs and benefits related to accelerating W-2 deadlines. The full costs will not be known until IRS analyzes details regarding how the agency would implement this change (e.g., the thresholds IRS uses to match W-2s will influence the number of W-2 mismatches due to IDT refund fraud or false positives, where legitimate returns are flagged during matching). Similarly, IRS does not have a well-developed estimate of the magnitude of the benefits of pre-refund W-2 matching. Treasury developed revenue projections for moving all information reporting deadlines, but did not develop projections specific to the W-2 deadline. While IRS has a basis for estimating the revenue protected from pre-refund matching (from its *Taxonomy*), other benefits—such as employer savings from fewer queries from IRS—may be harder to estimate.

- **SSA**. Moving the deadline to January 31 would create logistical and technical challenges for SSA. As previously discussed, SSA officials told us that moving the deadline to January 31 or earlier would require shifting its software development cycle because SSA's computer experts are working on another system during that timeframe; however, the computer experts are available to implement an accelerated W-2 filing date of February 29. If concurrent changes in the e-file threshold are not made, SSA may also incur administrative costs, should the number of W-2 corrections increase or a processing backlog occur (see next section for details).

- **Third parties**. The costs and benefits to employers and payroll providers have not been quantified. SSA officials stated that moving any W-2 deadline (other than the current e-file deadline of March 31) involves a degree of risk that cannot be quantified at present. They recommended surveying employers and payroll providers to better understand the impact of shortening or eliminating the time gap between when W-2s must be provided to employees and when they must be provided to SSA.

Estimating the costs and benefits of options to accelerate W-2 deadlines and to conduct earlier W-2 matching is consistent with IRS's strategic plan, which includes objectives to strengthen refund fraud prevention through the use of third-party data and to use analytics for timely, informed decision making.[28] It is also consistent with *Standards for Internal Control in the Federal Government*, which calls for IRS management to design and implement internal controls within its programs based on the related costs and benefits.[29] However, without better analysis of the costs and benefits of options for implementing accelerated W-2 deadlines and pre-refund matching, Congress does not have the information needed to consider Treasury's proposal and deliberate the merits of making such a significant change.

Other Policy Changes May Be Needed to Implement Earlier, Pre-refund W-2 Matching

Agency officials and third-party stakeholders we spoke to noted that other policy changes may also be needed in concert with moving W-2 deadlines. This is because W-2 matching is part of a much larger tax-administration system that provides IRS with information needed to help verify the identity, employment, and earnings of taxpayers. These changes could include lowering the e-file threshold for employers, delaying refunds, or delaying the start of the filing season. IRS has not yet undertaken efforts to understand the full costs of implementing earlier, pre-refund W-2 matching, and the costs associated with these other changes.

Lowering the E-File Threshold for Employers

Because of the additional time and resources associated with processing paper W-2s submitted by employers, SSA officials told us that a change in the e-file threshold would be needed to sufficiently increase the number of e-filed W-2s. Reducing the e-file threshold would allow IRS to obtain timely, accurate data from a significant number of employers and would

---

[28]IRS, *Strategic Plan: FY2014-2017*.

[29]GAO/AIMD-00-21.3.1.

enhance the benefits IRS could obtain from the accelerated W-2 deadline and pre-refund W-2 matching. Currently, employers who file 250 or more W-2s annually must e-file those forms.[30] Low-volume filers (filing fewer than 250 information returns annually) can file on paper, and for tax year 2011 these employers sent about 27.6 million paper W-2s (13 percent of all W-2s filed), according to IRS data. Because of the additional time SSA needs to process paper W-2s before sending them to IRS, changes in the e-file threshold would be necessary for earlier W-2 deadlines to have the intended effect. Without a change in the e-file threshold, backlogs in paper W-2s could result in IRS receiving W-2 data after the end of the filing season. For example, SSA officials said they can have a large backlog of paper W-2s and can process some paper W-2s as late as August or September. Having more e-filed W-2s would speed processing time for SSA (as compared to paper W-2 processing time) and would enable IRS to receive a larger percentage of W-2 data earlier, according to SSA officials.

More than 4.5 million establishments have fewer than 10 employees,[31] and SSA officials estimated that the e-file threshold would need to be reduced to 5 to 10 information returns for the change to result in a meaningful increase in the number of e-filed W-2s. Many states have already implemented lower e-file thresholds. According to the American Payroll Association, 19 states, the District of Columbia, and Puerto Rico have a W-2 e-file threshold that is lower than IRS's information return requirement.[32]

Two of the three payroll and information reporting associations we interviewed said lowering the e-file threshold would not create problems for most employers.[33] An organization representing small businesses was generally supportive of lowering the e-file threshold, but also noted that a minority of small businesses may oppose a threshold reduction. However, there are ways to mitigate the burden on small businesses, including

---

[30]26 C.F.R. § 301.6011-2(b)(2). IRS is generally prohibited from requiring those filing fewer than 250 returns annually to e-file. 26 U.S.C. § 6011(e)(2)(A).

[31]According to 2011 U.S. Census Bureau data.

[32]American Payroll Association, *PayState Update*, vol. 16, iss. 2 (2014). Thresholds vary by state. For example, Connecticut and Virginia mandate e-filing for all employers. Other states require e-filing for more than 11-100 information returns.

[33]The third association did not comment on the e-file threshold during our interview.

implementing a gradual reduction in the threshold and/or allowing employers to file for hardship waivers.[34] Additionally, small employers can e-file W-2s at no cost through SSA's web application, Business Services Online.

In addition to contributing to the IRS's ability to verify employment information on tax returns, lowering the e-file threshold could reduce administrative costs for SSA. Based on fiscal year 2013 data, SSA officials stated that an e-filed W-2 costs about $0.002 to process, while a paper W-2 costs about $0.53 to transcribe and process.[35] Moreover, SSA officials said it is more difficult to ensure data quality with paper W-2s, as transcription errors can occur while processing paper W-2s.

Treasury recently requested that Congress expand legal authority to allow a reduction of the 250-return e-filing threshold for a broad set of information returns, including W-2s.[36] According to Treasury, benefits such as enhancing taxpayer compliance, improving IRS service to taxpayers, and modernizing tax administration make this change worthwhile. For example, expanding e-filing will help IRS focus its audit activities, as IRS will receive information in a useable form, according to Treasury. The cost savings described above, as well as compliance and other benefits, could be realized before Congress decides on whether to accelerate W-2 deadlines (as proposed by Treasury). The change would support IRS's strategic objectives to encourage compliance while minimizing costs and taxpayer burden.[37] In addition, increasing e-filing is consistent with internal controls, which require that information be recorded and communicated to management and others within the entity who need it and in a form and within a timeframe that enables them to carry out their internal control and other responsibilities.[38] For an entity to run and control its operations, it must have relevant, reliable, and timely communications relating to internal as well as external events.

---

[34]IRS made similar gradual threshold reductions when implementing e-filing requirements for paid preparers.

[35]We did not verify SSA's estimates.

[36]Treasury, *General Explanations of the Administration's Fiscal Year 2015 Revenue Proposals.*

[37]IRS, *Strategic Plan: FY2014-2017.*

[38]GAO/AIMD-00-21.3.1.

Implementing a lower e-filing threshold would have the ancillary benefit (described above) of supporting pre-refund matching.

Delaying Refunds and Delaying the Start of the Filing Season

In conjunction with other strategies such as earlier filing of W-2s, delaying the filing season or delaying refunds would provide more time for IRS to receive W-2s, conduct pre-refund matching, and identify IDT refund fraud, according to IRS and third-party officials.[39] IRS could delay the start of the filing season—the date IRS begins to process tax returns—but changing IRS's obligation to issue refunds within 45 days of the due date of the return would require a statutory amendment.[40] Both changes would have costs associated with educating taxpayers about the changes and potential costs to taxpayers who receive refunds later (discussed below). In our discussions with third parties about ways to prevent IDT refund fraud, 10 of the 22 groups we interviewed—ranging from financial institution associations to software companies to payroll associations—specifically suggested the option of delaying refunds or delaying the filing season until IRS could match W-2 data to tax returns.[41]

Delaying refunds is likely to burden taxpayers, according to IRS and third-party officials. Taxpayers who file early and who are financially dependent on a refund, such as low-income taxpayers receiving refundable credits, could be burdened. For example, according to the National Taxpayer Advocate, delayed refunds would have a detrimental effect on low-income taxpayers who use their tax refunds to pay winter utility bills.[42] According to our analysis, the changes would also result in a permanent shift in the annual cycle of refunds on which some taxpayers depend. Once the change is made, the time interval between annual refunds will be the same length as it is now; however, during the first year of implementation,

---

[39]Currently, IRS delays refunds for suspicious returns. For example, IRS's Taxpayer Protection Program reviews suspicious returns flagged by IRS's identity theft filters and requires taxpayers to confirm their identities before IRS issues the refund.

[40]The start of the filing season is typically in mid January, although IRS has delayed the start date of the filing season in the past, such as in 2013 and 2014.

[41]In our semistructured interviews, we did not specifically ask all 22 groups about the options of delaying refunds or delaying the filing season. Ten groups discussed delaying refunds or the filing season as a potential way for IRS to combat IDT refund fraud.

[42]National Taxpayer Advocate, *2013 Annual Report to Congress*, Vol. II.

that interval may be increased by several months. This additional waiting time in the first year could be burdensome for some taxpayers; however, there should be no added burden in subsequent years (i.e. the interval between refunds will be approximately 12 months in those later years).[43]

Weaknesses in Third-Party Partnership Programs Limit Post-Refund Fraud Detection

Through its external leads programs, IRS collaborates with financial institutions, software companies, prepaid card companies, and other third parties. These partnerships provide valuable information about emerging IDT trends and fraudulent returns that have passed through IRS's prevention and detection systems. External leads help IRS identify fraudulent refunds and understand emerging trends in IDT refund fraud and other refund fraud. According to IRS officials, the agency has used third-party leads to improve detection of IDT refund fraud.[44] Between January 1, 2014 and May 31, 2014, IRS reported that more than 350 sources sent IRS successful leads for nearly 94,000 taxpayer accounts: these leads were for all types of refund fraud including, but not limited to, IDT refund fraud.[45] IRS reported that financial institutions returned $214.8 million in fraudulent refunds during this period.

Communicating with third parties is consistent with IRS's strategic plan objective to implement a robust enterprise risk management program by establishing routine reporting procedures to inform external stakeholders about operational risks.[46] Also, it is consistent with internal controls, which require relevant, reliable, and timely communications relating to external events.[47] As such, management should ensure there are adequate

---

[43]IRS has a legal obligation to pay interest on refunds issued after 45 days from the due date of the tax return, and this requirement would apply to refund delays associated with pre-refund matching and IDT refund fraud detection. Taxpayers who currently receive their refunds prior to the 45-day deadline may incur opportunity costs to the extent they would not be able to accrue interest on the refund during the time period between the date they currently receive their refund and the 45-day deadline.

[44]According to IRS officials, IRS has received many suggestions from third parties. When deciding whether to implement these suggestions, officials consider factors such as budget, operational, and administrative constraints.

[45]IRS does not distinguish between leads based on suspicion of IDT refund fraud or other types of fraud.

[46]IRS, *Strategic Plan: FY2014-2017*.

[47]GAO/AIMD-00-21.3.1.

means of communicating with external stakeholders and of obtaining information from them that could help IRS achieve its goal of reducing IDT refund fraud.

Disclosure constraints limit what IRS can share. Section 6103 of the Internal Revenue Code limits the types of information IRS can share with external parties, even for fraudulent returns.[48] However, section 6103 does not limit IRS's ability to share general information about how to manage IDT refund fraud or emerging fraud trends. Disclosure of individual taxpayer information could be prevented by aggregating information so that no individual taxpayers could be identified. IRS officials told us that aggregated feedback to third parties may be possible, as long as a sufficient number of leads are discussed.

IRS feedback to third parties is limited. While IRS's feedback differs by external leads program, third parties receive limited feedback across both programs.[49] Eight of the eleven financial institution and tax software associations/companies we interviewed said that IRS provides little to no feedback in response to leads sent through the External Leads Program or the Opt-In Program, or they told us they requested additional feedback from IRS. Furthermore, IRS officials told us that the agency has received millions of leads from software companies, but while IRS makes an effort to examine and address the highest priority leads (e.g., high refund dollars), IRS has not analyzed or provided feedback about many of these leads because it does not have the resources to do so. Without accurate, timely, and actionable feedback, external parties do not know if the leads they provide to IRS are useful. Five of these eleven financial institution associations and tax software associations/companies volunteered that

---

[48]Tax returns and other information submitted to and, in some cases, generated by IRS, are confidential and protected from disclosure, except as specifically authorized by statute. 26 U.S.C. § 6103. Section 6103 protections apply equally to all tax returns and tax information that IRS receives, and it has no exceptions for fraudulent returns. In instances where a fraudulent return is under investigation, section 6103 allows IRS to share the minimum amount of tax return information necessary with financial institutions to facilitate the return of a fraudulent refund to IRS. In cases where financial institutions have rejected direct deposit refunds as part of the Opt-In Program, section 6103 does not allow IRS to share specific tax information with the financial institution.

[49]For leads submitted by financial institutions through the External Leads Program, IRS contacts the institutions to request that a suspicious refund be returned to IRS, thereby indicating some information about whether the lead helped to identify fraud. In contrast, IRS cannot provide similar feedback to financial institutions participating in the Opt-In Program because of legal restrictions.

they are not able to assess their success in identifying IDT refund fraud, or to improve their own detection tools.[50] Useful feedback may include aggregated information about the share of each institution's leads that helped to identify suspicious returns and other information about IDT refund fraud trends. This type of aggregated information would also comply with section 6103 disclosure requirements.

IRS's general and aggregated feedback is limited to particular groups. IRS shares general information about high-level schemes and IDT refund fraud trends during meetings with BITS, the technology policy division of the Financial Services Roundtable.[51] However, financial institutions that are not part of that organization may not have the opportunity to learn from these discussions.[52] In addition, IRS officials said they provide aggregated data about leads received to tax software companies that request the information, but companies that do not request the information may not receive this feedback.

IRS does not use metrics for tracking external leads. To provide aggregated feedback by institution, IRS would need to begin tracking this information. IRS officials said they have not implemented metrics by institution because of a lack of resources. While IRS compiles information—including the total number of external lead sources, leads submitted, and associated refund dollars—the agency does not use the information to develop metrics to track leads by the submitting third party. For the External Leads Program, IRS officials told us that while IRS monitors the volume of leads and associated refund dollars to assess accomplishments and program value, it does not use metrics to monitor and follow up on leads, including the tracking of leads by the third party

---

[50]In our semistructured interviews, we asked an open question about the extent to which IRS provided feedback. The five groups volunteered this particular impact.

[51]According to a BITS official, the Financial Services Roundtable represents the largest integrated financial services companies providing banking, insurance payment and investment products and services to the American consumer. BITS addresses emerging technology and operational opportunities for the financial services industry, helping members manage risk, particularly in cybersecurity, fraud reduction, vendor management, and critical infrastructure protection. BITS is not an acronym. At one time, BITS stood for "Banking Industry Technology Secretariat." However, with financial modernization and the emergence of integrated financial services companies, that term is no longer used.

[52]According to a BITS official, this information is available upon request through BITS for any financial institutions that are not its members. However, financial institutions need to know this information is available through BITS in order to request it.

that submitted them. In addition, IRS officials said while IRS provides some overall data for the Opt-In Program, it does not track this information by financial institution. Because IRS does not track external leads by institution, it cannot use this information to improve IDT refund fraud programs or to provide feedback to third parties about the effectiveness of their leads.

Strengthening IRS's partnerships with third parties would require IRS to expend resources analyzing leads and providing feedback to third parties. These costs could vary, depending on the systems involved and the level of feedback IRS provides. IRS has some of the information needed to track leads in this way. For example, spreadsheets submitted through the External Leads Program contain the institutions' names, so entirely new data collection systems may not be needed. Our past work has shown that developing metrics to track external leads by submitting party is consistent with practices that enhance the use of performance information, such as communicating that information frequently and effectively.[53] In addition, tracking external leads would support IRS's strategic goal of supporting effective tax administration by providing timely information to external partners in the tax community.[54] Metrics would allow IRS to communicate information to specific third parties, who could then adapt their own IDT detection tools. Given the millions of dollars in refund fraud returned by financial institutions in the first five months of 2014, even a modest increase in IDT refunds returned due to institution-specific feedback may be worth the investment of tracking external leads.

Conclusions

IDT refund fraud is a large problem: IRS estimates it issued at least $5.2 billion in fraudulent IDT refunds in filing season 2013. Given the size and scope of IDT refund fraud, additional bold and innovative steps are needed from Congress and IRS. For IRS to successfully combat IDT refund fraud, it will need to develop heightened awareness in its understanding of emerging trends, and in its ability to leverage both internal and external resources. While there is no "silver bullet" available to resolve the problem, developing strategies that focus on both preventing IDT refund fraud and resolving it can help IRS respond to this

---

[53]GAO, *Managing for Results: Enhancing Agency Use of Performance Information for Management Decision Making,* GAO-05-927 (Washington, D.C.: Sept. 9, 2005).

[54]IRS, *Strategic Plan: FY2014-2017,* (Washington, D.C.: 2014).

evolving threat. These strategies are likely to include constantly adapting and strengthening present defenses while also developing new strategies for both electronic and paper returns that stop IDT refund fraud at all stages of return processing.

Given the billions in dollars of successful IDT refund fraud, IRS must strive to stay one or more steps ahead of identity thieves, or the risk of issuing fraudulent IDT refunds could grow. Staying ahead of identity thieves will require a significant resource investment from IRS as it strengthens and develops new tools. Accelerating the W-2 deadline to January 31—as proposed by Treasury—would provide a powerful tool for IRS to detect and prevent IDT refund fraud. At the same time, the full costs and benefits are not known because IRS has not considered how it would implement pre-refund matching using W-2 data. The burden this would impose on employers, the costs to IRS for systems changes, and the likely need for other changes (such as increased e-filing) means this step should not be taken without an informed discussion among all stakeholders, including Congress. Further, taxpayers' expectations about the filing season and when they can anticipate receiving refunds may need to shift. Also, IRS has not fully leveraged third parties, having provided only limited feedback on the IDT refund leads third parties are submitting and offering limited general information on IDT refund fraud trends. However, to provide this information, IRS will need metrics to track external leads by the third party that submitted them, which it currently does not have. While the cost of providing third-party feedback could vary depending on the level of feedback IRS provides, third-party leads returned hundreds of millions of dollars in all refund fraud to the IRS in 2014, and are a valuable information resource about fraudulent returns that have bypassed IRS's prevention and detection systems.

Matters for Congressional Consideration

Congress should consider providing the Secretary of the Treasury with the regulatory authority to lower the threshold for electronic filing of W-2s from 250 returns annually to between 5 to 10 returns, as appropriate.

Recommendations for Executive Action

We recommend the Commissioner of Internal Revenue fully assess the costs and benefits of accelerating W-2 deadlines and provide information to Congress on

- the IRS systems and work processes that will need to be adjusted to accommodate earlier, pre-refund matching of W-2s and then identify timeframes for when these changes could be made;

- potential impacts on taxpayers, IRS, SSA, and third parties; and

- what other changes will be needed (such as delaying the start of the filing season or delaying refunds) to ensure IRS can match tax returns to W-2 data before issuing refunds.

We recommend that the Commissioner of Internal Revenue take the following two actions to provide timely, accurate, and actionable feedback to all relevant lead-generating third parties:

- provide aggregated information on (1) the success of external party leads in identifying suspicious returns and (2) emerging trends (pursuant to section 6103 restrictions); and

- develop a set of metrics to track external leads by the submitting third party.

Agency Comments and Our Evaluation

We provided a draft of this product to IRS and SSA for review and comment. In its written comments, reproduced in appendix III, IRS neither agreed nor disagreed with our recommendations. IRS stated that it is determining how potential corrective actions align with available resources and IRS priorities before deciding whether to implement the recommendations. With regard to our first set of recommendations, IRS acknowledged that accelerating W-2 deadlines or delaying the tax filing season represents a significant change to tax administration. IRS stated that in order to determine the best course of action, Congress needs an understanding of the costs and benefits for IRS and other stakeholders. With regard to our second set of recommendations, IRS stated that information sharing, as permitted under the law—such as providing feedback to third parties—fosters good working relationships and promotes ongoing program improvements. IRS provided technical comments that we incorporated, as appropriate.

We recognize the need for IRS to assess its priorities given the fiscal constraints it faces. We previously reported that since fiscal year 2010, IRS has absorbed approximately $900 million in budget cuts while facing increasing workloads as a result of legislative mandates and priority programs, such as work related to the Patient Protection and Affordable Care Act.[55] Even with these constraints and other potentially competing priorities, we believe the size of the IDT problem warrants additional action now. Pre-refund matching of W-2 data is one option that IRS agrees has the potential to prevent a substantial portion of the estimated $5.2 billion in IDT refunds paid in filing season 2013. However, such a change may require a significant resource investment by IRS as well as impact taxpayers and employers. Without better information about the benefits and costs of such a significant change, Congress cannot make an informed decision about implementing it. With respect to our recommendations regarding the External Leads Program, IRS highlighted the fact that the program has generated more than $2.3 billion in refunds returned to the U.S. Treasury from 2010 to 2014. Given that IRS already has some of the information needed to better track external lead results, IRS should be able to control the costs of implementing our recommendations.

In its written comments, reproduced in appendix IV, SSA stated that its implementation of a redesigned Annual Wage Reporting system for processing W-2s in January 2015 and W-2cs in January 2016 will position the agency to support an accelerated W-2 deadline as well as support lowering the threshold for e-filing W-2s. SSA also said that it transmits wage data to IRS immediately upon receiving electronic W-2s. Paper W-2s require manual handling and therefore have a significantly longer processing time. SSA also recommended that IRS consider the impact of Form 1099 reporting in making decisions to accelerate the W-2 reporting and change IRS business processes. SSA also provided technical comments that we incorporated, as appropriate.

As agreed with your offices, unless you publicly announce the contents of this report earlier, we plan no further distribution until 30 days from the report date. At that time, we will send copies to the Commissioner of

---

[55]GAO, *Internal Revenue Service: Absorbing Budget Cuts Has Resulted in Significant Staffing Declines and Uneven Budget Performance*, GAO-14-534R (Washington, D.C.: Apr. 21, 2014).

Internal Revenue. In addition, the report will be available at no charge on the GAO website at http://www.gao.gov.

If you or your staff have any questions about this report, please contact me at (202) 512-9910 or whitej@gao.gov. Contact points for our Offices of Congressional Relations and Public Affairs may be found on the last page of this report. GAO staff who made key contributions to this report are listed in appendix V.

James R. White
Director, Tax Issues
Strategic Issues

Appendix I: IRS *Identity Theft Taxonomy* Limitations

IRS developed the *Identity Theft Taxonomy* (*Taxonomy*) to monitor the volume of identity theft (IDT) refund fraud attempts and assess the impact of its IDT defenses over time, among other reasons. The *Taxonomy* is a matrix of IDT refund fraud categories that estimate the amount of *identified* IDT refund fraud IRS prevented or recovered, as well as the *identified* IDT refund fraud IRS paid. The estimates are based on IRS's administrative records of known IDT refund fraud (e.g., data on the number of duplicate returns or returns detected by identity theft filters). The *Taxonomy* also estimates likely identity theft by identifying returns with the characteristics of IDT refund fraud, which are found when IRS matches returns to W-2 and other information return data after the tax filing season. The *Taxonomy* is a valuable step toward inventorying available IDT refund fraud data and assessing the performance of IRS's IDT refund fraud defenses. However, we identified limitations in the *Taxonomy*, specifically

- **Taxonomy estimates are preliminary.** After we provided a draft for comment, IRS officials stated that the *Taxonomy* estimates are preliminary, as they are updating their analysis using information return matching to identify likely returns where IRS paid IDT refunds. They anticipate their estimates for IDT refunds paid will increase somewhat (perhaps by $0.6 billion), but an updated *Taxonomy* estimate was not completed in time for us to include in this report.

- **Using administrative records could result in imprecise estimates.** *Taxonomy* estimates could be imprecise because the returns identified may not accurately represent the true universe of IDT refund fraud. If only certain kinds of criminals (or fraudsters) are more likely to be detected by IRS defenses, IRS records on detected IDT refund fraud may not accurately represent all individuals attempting to commit IDT refund fraud.

- **Certain *Taxonomy* estimates are based on assumptions using the characteristics of past IDT refund fraud.** While the assumptions are based on IRS's research from known cases and appear reasonable, we could not verify the accuracy and comprehensiveness of these assumptions. This is because the accuracy of the *Taxonomy* estimates is largely based on whether the estimate includes all true IDT refund fraud returns and excludes all legitimate returns. IRS officials acknowledged their estimates for returns flagged during information return matching could include legitimate returns that are not actual IDT refund fraud. For example, the estimate could include returns flagged due to taxpayer or employer error or other non-IDT fraud by taxpayers (e.g., the taxpayer deliberately enters false information on his tax return to obtain a larger refund). Changes in these assumptions can substantially affect the estimates, but this uncertainty is not reflected in IRS's *Taxonomy* estimates for filing season 2013 (e.g., IRS does not present a range of estimates based on differing assumptions).

- **IRS's *Taxonomy* underestimates the number of IDT refund fraud returns and refund amounts for some IDT categories.** IRS's estimate of IDT refunds paid is based on duplicate returns, information return mismatches, and criminal investigations identified after the refunds are paid. However, for cases where there are no duplicate returns, information returns, or criminal investigations associated with a tax return, IRS has been unable to estimate the amount of IDT refund fraud. IRS officials have considered using surveys to estimate unidentified IDT refund fraud, but have not been able to come up with a survey method that would avoid significant taxpayer burden.

- **IRS's *Taxonomy* overestimates the number of IDT refund fraud returns and refund amounts for some IDT categories.** For example, IRS's estimates for "refunds protected" include refunds returned to IRS as a result of external leads. However, IRS data on external leads do not distinguish whether the type of fraud was IDT refund fraud or some other type of fraud. Our analysis of the *Taxonomy* found that IRS did not adjust its estimate to account for other types of refund fraud.

- **Methodology changes and other factors prevent comparisons between filing seasons 2012 and 2013 estimates.** For filing season 2012, IRS estimates it prevented or recovered about $21.6 billion (71 percent) of the estimated IDT refunds and paid $8.9 billion (29 percent). Comparing filing season 2012 and 2013 estimates is problematic because it is unclear whether the changes are due to methodological changes, such as using different data sources or changing the criteria for querying data. IRS officials said they update their methodology to better reflect evolving IDT refund fraud schemes and improve the accuracy of *Taxonomy* estimates, although they attempt to use consistent definitions to promote comparability of estimates across years. In addition, it is unclear whether changes are due to overall changes in fraud patterns, such as an increase or decrease in fraud attempts; improvements in IRS IDT defenses; or identity thieves' ability to file returns using schemes IRS has not yet learned to detect.

It is likely that IRS's estimates of the IDT refund fraud for filing seasons 2012 and 2013 will continue to evolve as IRS improves the *Taxonomy* methodology. For example, during the course of our audit, we found that IRS's methodology for counting returns did not include two categories of duplicate returns that should have been included in the estimates. IRS officials estimated that including these returns would increase IRS's original 2013 estimates of refunds paid out by $0.47 billion, from $4.75 billion to $5.22 billion in filing season 2013.

Appendix II: Objectives, Scope, and Methodology

This report examines (1) what the Internal Revenue Service (IRS) knows about the extent of identity theft (IDT) refund fraud and (2) what additional actions IRS can take to combat IDT refund fraud using third-party information (for example, from employers and financial institutions). As described earlier, the report discusses IDT refund fraud and not employment fraud, unless otherwise noted.

To understand what IRS knows about the extent of IDT refund fraud, we reviewed IRS's *Identity Theft Taxonomy (Taxonomy)*, which estimates the amount of IDT refund fraud that IRS is, and is not, preventing. We conducted manual data testing for obvious errors and compared underlying data to IRS's *Refund Fraud & Identity Theft Global Report*. We confirmed *Taxonomy* components where we had data available to cross check. We also interviewed IRS officials to better understand the methodology used to create the estimates and the changes in methodology, data sources, and assumptions across the years of data available. For details on our findings about the *Taxonomy* components we evaluated, see appendix I.

To identify opportunities to improve IRS's IDT refund fraud efforts, we reviewed *Internal Revenue Manual* sections detailing IRS's Identity Protection Program and IRS documentation for its External Leads Program, the Opt-In Program, and other third-party efforts. We also reviewed Treasury's legislative proposals and Congressional testimony of IRS officials. We interviewed officials and reviewed documentation from the Social Security Administration (SSA) and several of the third parties shown in table 1 below, where applicable. We selected a nonprobability sample of 22 associations and stakeholders with differing positions and characteristics to help ensure our analysis covered a variety of viewpoints, based on IRS documentation and suggestions, our prior work, and other information. For example, to select associations representing financial institutions, we considered, among other factors, the size and type of institutions they represented (e.g., large or small banks, credit unions, and prepaid debit card companies). Because we used a nonprobability sample, the views of these associations are not generalizable to all potential third parties.

Table 1: List of Third Parties Interviewed

Software and Analytics Companies	1. Equifax
	2. H&R Block[a]
	3. Intuit
	4. LexisNexis
	5. SAS
Tax Software and Return Preparer Associations and Advisory Committees	6. American Coalition for Taxpayer Rights
	7. American Institute of CPAs
	8. Electronic Tax Administration Advisory Committee
	9. Free File Alliance
Financial Institution and Payment Associations	10. American Bankers Association
	11. BITS[b]
	12. The Clearing House
	13. Credit Union National Association[c]
	14. NACHA – The Electronic Payments Association
	15. National Association of Federal Credit Unions
	16. Network Branded Prepaid Card Association
Payroll, Information Reporting, and Small Business Associations	17. American Payroll Association
	18. Information Reporting Program Advisory Committee
	19. National Federation of Independent Businesses
	20. Reporting Agent Forum
Others	21. Federation of Tax Administrators
	22. National Taxpayer Advocate

Source: GAO. | GAO-14-633

[a]Also offers in-person tax preparation and banking services.

[b]Technology policy division of the Financial Services Roundtable. BITS is not an acronym. At one time, BITS stood for "Banking Industry Technology Secretariat." However, with financial modernization and the emergence of integrated financial services companies, that term is no longer used.

[c]Provided written comments.

When possible, we used a standard set of questions in interviewing these associations and summarized the results of the semistructured interviews. However, as needed, we also sought perspectives on additional questions tailored to these associations' expertise and sought their opinions on key issues. We then discussed these options with officials from IRS offices, including (1) Privacy, Government Liaison, and Disclosure and (2) Return Integrity and Correspondence Services to determine the feasibility of various options and the challenges of pursuing them.

To describe the timing of refunds issued compared to W-2 submissions,
we analyzed SSA data for filing season 2013 and IRS data for filing
season 2012.[1] SSA provided data on the cumulative number of W-2s it
received for filing season 2013. We assessed the reliability of SSA data
by performing electronic tests to identify obvious errors and discussing
the data with SSA officials. We found the data were sufficiently reliable for
the purposes of providing contextual information on when SSA receives
W-2s.

For IRS data, we used analysis developed for GAO-13-515 on the timing
of W-2s and tax returns. This analysis obtained data from IRS's
Compliance Data Warehouse (CDW) database, which provides a variety
of tax return, enforcement, compliance, and other data.[2] In analyzing
when tax returns were received by IRS, we used the cycle posting date
(when IRS posts tax return data to the master file), as it represents when
the tax return data are available for matching. Officials noted that IRS
must refine the data prior to posting to IRS systems. This may include
identifying and correcting incomplete or inaccurate data before posting
the data to IRS systems. We assessed the reliability of CDW data by (1)
performing electronic or manual testing of required data elements to
identify obvious errors, (2) reviewing existing information about the data
and the system that produced them, and (3) interviewing agency officials
knowledgeable about the data. We determined that the data were
sufficiently reliable for the purposes of this report.

We conducted this performance audit from May 2014 to August 2014 in
accordance with generally accepted government auditing standards.
Those standards require that we plan and perform the audit to obtain
sufficient, appropriate evidence to provide a reasonable basis for our
findings and conclusions based on our audit objectives. We believe that
the evidence obtained provides a reasonable basis for our findings and
conclusions based on our audit objectives.

---

[1]Our analysis of IRS data on the timing of information returns is from a previous report
(GAO-13-515).

[2]Our analysis of IRS data is based on return data extracted from CDW April 17, 2013. For
our previous review, IRS officials reviewed our information return counts as of this date
and confirmed that our data were substantially the same as their counts at that time.

Appendix III: Comments from the Internal Revenue Service

DEPARTMENT OF THE TREASURY
INTERNAL REVENUE SERVICE
WASHINGTON, D.C. 20224

DEPUTY COMMISSIONER

Mr. James R. White
Director, Tax Issues
U.S. Government Accountability Office
441 G Street, N.W.
Washington, DC 20548

Dear Mr. White:

I have reviewed your draft report entitled *IDENTITY THEFT: Additional Actions Could Help IRS Combat the Large, Evolving Threat of Refund Fraud,* and appreciate your acknowledgment of the actions we have taken in recent years to detect and prevent Identity Theft (IDT) refund fraud at the time returns are filed, and processes we have implemented to recover refunds identified as potentially fraudulent by external partners. The IRS Identity Theft Taxonomy (Taxonomy) project and the continued growth of the External Leads program are critical components of our strategy to address and stop refund fraud attributable to IDT.

As noted in the report, the schemes employed by those individuals attempting to commit IDT refund fraud are constantly evolving and employing new tactics, presenting unique challenges to the IRS in combatting the fraud. The Taxonomy project is a vital component of our strategy to address these fraud attempts because it can provide analysis to identify the remaining trends for undetected identity theft and assist us in refining our future IDT filters to identify those returns with a high potential for fraud, while significantly reducing the likelihood of ensnaring the return of a legitimate taxpayer due to overly broad filtering criteria. A significant amount of effort has been invested in development of the Taxonomy, and we believe it represents a significant step forward in effectively stopping IDT refund fraud.

The External Leads program is a partnership the IRS established with financial institutions and other government agencies in an effort to combat IDT. Since its inception, the program has grown from 10 partners in 2010, to 359 partners in 2014, who have identified potentially fraudulent refunds and, from 2010 through 2014, returned 699,901 refunds determined to actually be fraudulent, representing more than $2.3 billion returned to the United States Treasury. As the program has grown, we have recognized the need for comprehensive metrics to evaluate the program's performance, and the need for a strong communications strategy with our partners to ensure continued success. We have taken actions to address both needs.

Another process vital to the detection of refund fraud, as well as tax administration in general, is the ability of the IRS to use information provided by third party payors to

2

verify and corroborate information presented on income tax returns. The ability to
narrow or close the gap between the time tax returns are filed and the time at which
third-party information is available for use by the IRS is a concept with the potential to
yield significant benefits to the government and to taxpayers, but can also impose
burdens that must be quantified and carefully considered by policy makers.
Implementing such a change to the tax system would be a substantial undertaking, and
we agree that the Congress needs to have a well-informed understanding of the costs
and benefits in order to determine the best course of action.

Responses to your specific recommendations are enclosed. If you have any questions,
please contact Jodi L. Patterson, Director, Return Integrity and Correspondence
Services, Wage and Investment Division, at (404) 338-8961.

Sincerely,

John M. Dalrymple
Deputy Commissioner for
Services and Enforcement

Enclosure

Enclosure

Recommendations for Executive Action

Recommendation 1
We recommend the Commissioner of Internal Revenue fully assess the costs and
benefits of accelerating W-2 deadlines and provide information to Congress on

1. The IRS systems and work processes that will need to be adjusted to
   accommodate earlier, pre-refund matching of W-2s and then identify timeframes
   for when these changes could be made;

2. Identify potential impacts on taxpayers, IRS, SSA, and third parties; and

3. Determine what other changes will be needed (such as delaying the start of the
   filing season or delaying refunds) to ensure IRS can match tax returns to W-2
   data before issuing refunds.

Comment
Accelerating the filing deadline of Form W-2, *Wage and Tax Statement*, or delaying the
filing season, represents a significant environmental change in the administration of
individual income taxation and can substantially impact affected stakeholders. We
recognize the importance of informing policy makers of not only the requisite systemic
changes and resource needs within the IRS for effectively responding to an accelerated
filing deadline, but also providing a discussion of the costs and benefits to be realized
by others outside the organization. To supplement the research that has already been
undertaken by the IRS on this subject, we will evaluate the relationship an accelerated
filing deadline initiative will have with existing priorities and proceed accordingly in
providing an analysis to Congress.

Recommendation 2
We recommend that the Commissioner of Internal Revenue take the following two
actions to provide timely, accurate, and actionable feedback to all relevant lead-
generating third parties:

1. Provide aggregated information on (1) the success of external party leads in
   identifying suspicious returns and (2) emerging trends (pursuant to IRC section
   6103 restrictions); and

2. Develop a set of metrics to track external leads by the submitting third party.

Comment
We have performed an extensive amount of outreach and communication with our
External Leads program partners, and agree that sharing information, as permitted
under the law, fosters good working relationships and promotes ongoing improvements
in program efficiencies. The External Leads program has experienced a tremendous

2

amount of growth since 2010 and, as it matures, we are re-evaluating our reporting and performance metrics, and will use improvements in performance measurement to similarly improve the quality of the information we are able to share with our outside partners.

Appendix IV: Comments from the Social Security Administration

SOCIAL SECURITY
Office of the Commissioner

August 11, 2014

Mr. James R. White
Director, Tax Issues
Strategic Issues
United States Government Accountability Office
441 G Street, NW
Washington, DC 20548

Dear Mr. White:

Thank you for the opportunity to review the draft report, "IDENTITY THEFT: Additional Actions Could Help IRS Combat the Large, Evolving Threat of Refund Fraud" (GAO-14-633). We have enclosed our response to the audit report contents.

If you have any questions, please contact me at (410) 966-9014. Your staff may contact Gary S. Hatcher, our Senior Advisor for Records Management and Audit Liaison Staff, at (410) 965-0680.

Sincerely,

Katherine Thornton
Deputy Chief of Staff

Enclosure

SOCIAL SECURITY ADMINISTRATION   BALTIMORE, MD 21235-0001

**COMMENTS ON THE GOVERNMENT ACCOUNTABILITY OFFICE (GAO) DRAFT
REPORT, "IDENTITY THEFT: ADDITIONAL ACTIONS COULD HELP IRS
COMBAT THE LARGE, EVOLVING THREAT OF REFUND FRAUD" (GAO-14-633)**

General Comments

In describing our process for transmitting data to the Internal Revenue Service (IRS) on the
"Highlights Page," pages 15, 19, and 20, it is important to note that we transmit wage data to IRS
immediately upon receiving the reports. Beginning in late January, non-exception electronic
reports are typically processed overnight. Paper reports require manual handling and therefore
have a significantly longer processing time. Our peak time for processing electronic W-2s is
normally mid-February to mid-March, which coincides with the peak submission period for
employers to submit electronic W-2 data reports.

While GAO's report focuses on W-2 wage data reports, it is also important to note that W-2s are
not the only report matched electronically with tax returns annually in July. Other information
report such as form 1099 "Miscellaneous Income;" form(s) 1098 "Mortgage Interest,"
"Charitable Donation," "Student Loan Interest," and "Student Tuition;" and form K-1 "Partner's
Share of Income, Deductions, Credits, etc." also report income. The volume of reports on other
information returns is between four and five times greater than the of W-2 earnings information
reports. Given the volume and timing of the availability of those reports, the IRS will need to
consider the impact of 1099 reporting in making decisions to change its business process to
accelerate the W-2 reporting requirements during the peak tax filing season.

Our implementation of a redesigned Annual Wage Reporting system for processing
W-2s in January 2015 and W-2cs in January 2016 will position us to support an IRS earlier filing
deadline as well as support lowering the threshold for the required electronic filing.

TECHNICAL COMMENTS

Highlights page, last paragraph and page 23, line 9, our cost to process a paper W-2 is now $0.53
(not $0.33) and the cost remains $0.002 per e-filed W-2. Thus, the estimated administrative cost
savings shown on the Highlights page would be more than $0.52 (not $0.32).

Page 19, replace the last two sentences with the following, "SSA officials indicated that moving
deadlines to January 31 or earlier would require moving its software development cycle;
however, the computer experts are available to implement an accelerated filing date for W-2s of
February 29."

Page 20, 2nd bullet, replace the first two sentences with the following, "As previously discussed,
SSA officials indicated that moving deadlines to January 31 or earlier would require moving its
software development cycle; however, the computer experts are available to implement an
accelerated filing date for W-2s of February 29."

Page 22, 1st paragraph, last sentence, change to read, "Having more e-filed W-2s would speed
processing time for SSA (as compared to paper W-2 processing time) and enable IRS to receive
a larger percentage of W-2 data earlier."

Appendix V: GAO Contact and Staff Acknowledgments

GAO Contact	James R. White, (202) 512-9110 or whitej@gao.gov.
Staff Acknowledgments	In addition to the individual named above, Neil Pinney, Assistant Director; Shannon Finnegan, Analyst-in-Charge; Amy Bowser; Deirdre Duffy; Michele Fejfar; Timothy Guinane; Katharine Kairys; Donna Miller; Dae Park; and Ellen Rominger made key contributions to this report. Gary Bianchi, Nina Crocker, Mary Evans, Ron Jones, David Lewis, Paul Middleton, Susan E. Murphy, Sabine Paul, Sara Pelton, Julie Spetz, Jim Wozny, and John Zombro also provided assistance.

Related GAO Products

GAO. *Financial Audit: IRS's Fiscal Years 2013 and 2012 Financial Statements.* GAO-14-169. Washington, D.C.: December 12, 2013.

GAO. *Internal Revenue Service: 2013 Tax Filing Season Performance to Date and Budget Data.* GAO-13-541R. Washington, D.C.: April 15, 2013.

GAO. *Identity Theft: Total Extent of Refund Fraud Using Stolen Identities is Unknown.* GAO-13-132T. Washington, D.C.: November 29, 2012.

GAO. *Financial Audit: IRS's Fiscal Years 2012 and 2011 Financial Statements.* GAO-13-120. Washington, D.C.: November 9, 2012.

GAO. *Taxes and Identity Theft: Status of IRS Initiatives to Help Victimized Taxpayers.* GAO-11-721T. Washington, D.C.: June 2, 2011.

GAO. *Taxes and Identity Theft: Status of IRS Initiatives to Help Victimized Taxpayers.* GAO-11-674T. Washington, D.C.: May 25, 2011.

GAO. *Tax Administration: IRS Has Implemented Initiatives to Prevent, Detect, and Resolve Identity Theft-Related Problems, but Needs to Assess Their Effectiveness.* GAO-09-882. Washington, D.C.: September 8, 2009.